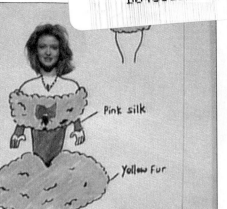

Pink silk

Yellow fur

de of
velvet
feathers.

dress made of
purple pink and
green tafetta.

RED HOT

Red hot certainly is
red hot, the clinging
velvet dress falls onto
the shoulders and shapes
the whole figure. The hat
influenced by the hot flame
in a burning fire, this also
has a velvet look to it.
The earrings are unusually
shaped to stand out. Red
lights are stunning and
create an unbroken line to
the figure, and to match, a
pair of shapely heeled
red velvet shoes.

CONTENTS

This edition published by Ringpress Books, by
arrangement with BBC Books, a division of BBC
Enterprises Ltd. Blue Peter is a registered trade
mark of the British Broadcasting Corporation.

Distributed by Ruskin Book Services Ltd.,
Adam House, Birmingham Rd., Kidderminster,
Worcs DY10 2SA. Tel (0562) 515151.

Biddy Baxter, Edward Barnes and **Lewis Bronze**
devised and wrote the **Blue Peter Book**

Step inside Blue Peter's 25th Book, and you won't be disappointed . . .

HELLO THERE!

W E'VE packed in lots of highlights of the year in which we turned thirty years old, visited the United States, Kampuchea, went Green and welcomed the seventeenth Blue Peter presenter to the programme.

He is John Leslie, the tallest presenter yet, and the first Scot to join the team. He's had an amazing introduction to the sort of busy life he can expect for the next few years. For his first film, Mark took him to a railway bridge over a gorge in Wales and introduced him to the hair-raising new sport of bridge-swinging. You can read about that adventure in this book as well as examine John's Datafile on page fifteen.

John is taking over from Mark, who has spent three fun years on Blue Peter. We are going to miss him in the studio, with his ability to burst into song whatever the excuse, and crack jokes. Everyone wishes him the best of luck in his future career.

This has been the year the programme said goodbye to its inspiration and guiding hand for the last twenty-seven years — Biddy Baxter. Biddy still keeps in touch, of course, and she hasn't left us entirely – as you can see if you look at the inside front cover of this book!

So eyes down for a good read. Don't miss the story of Caron's ice climb up Ben Nevis, nor Mark's hair-raising windmill ride!

Relive our adventures on the West Coast of America, and don't forget about our competition. This is your chance to win a rare prize — a visit to our studios at BBC Television Centre! Maybe we'll meet *you*!

Don't forget — Blue Peter is all about *your* ideas. Tell us what you think, especially if it's about what is happening to our surroundings. You might win one of our new Green Blue Peter Badges!

4

Do you recognise any of these photographs? They've all been on Blue Peter. Turn to page 60 for the answers.

BONNIE

WILLOW

GEORGE

ICE CLIMB

Baby it's cold outside: Caron and Stephen prepared for the worst.

Climbing a mountain in dry weather when the sun is shining is naturally a hazardous business. But the great mountains of the world are perpetually snow-capped, so no matter what time of year you choose, the final assault on the peak is going to be made in freezing cold and highly dangerous conditions.

The weather, once you pass 1,000 feet, can close in at any time, and it is weather that accounts for the majority of mountaineering disasters. Two of Blue Peter's great mountaineering friends, Mick Burke on Everest and Judy Tullis on K2, both died as a result of weather.

If you are a serious mountaineer you need to be able to survive in sub-zero temperatures and force ten blizzards while climbing up a wall of ice. I wouldn't actually class myself as a serious mountaineer, but the challenge of an ice climb was something I couldn't let go. So last winter I found myself at the foot of the snowy peak of Ben Nevis, the highest mountain in Britain, with Stephen Venables. Stephen was the first Briton to reach the summit of Mount Everest without oxygen, and lost three and a half toes from frostbite in the process. He is a tall, gangling, bespectacled man, very charming and jokey — he looked more like an overgrown student than a mountaineer. Once on the mountain he treated everything, no matter how difficult or dangerous, as a matter of routine, which gave me a feeling of instant confidence.

I had been standing-by for weeks to do this climb. It had been the mildest winter that anyone could remember, and snow, even in the North of Scotland, was a very scarce commodity. By March I had almost given up when Stephen telephoned from Scotland.

"The peak is covered, Caron, and the forecast is for more snow, so if you fancy a bit of ice climbing, now's the time."

"Oh good," I heard myself saying, and then I wondered if that was how I really felt.

The team for the climb was Stephen, his climbing partner Bill Longman, and me.

The mountaineering camera team was Max Sammett on camera and Gordon Forsyth on sound. This was going to be the kind of story where it is appropriate to say: "Every time you see me doing something terrifying, there is a camera crew doing something even more terrifying to get the shot." And the crew had set off up the mountain a few hours before us to get into position to film the climb. To save time we travelled to the foot of the mountain by helicopter, an unheard of luxury for Stephen whose mountaineering expeditions usually begin with a fortnight's foot slog to get to the place where the climbing begins.

Back to the Ice Age: Bill, Caron and Stephen on their way to the peak.

the snow for what felt like a couple of seconds, and then I lifted my head hoping to get a heartening glimpse of the sunlit peak, and saw a great white wall rolling down the mountain towards me.

"Uh-Uh — looks as though we're in for some Scottish weather," Stephen remarked. The next second we were in the middle of a white out. I could see nothing but whirling snow, and the temperature seemed to drop about 20 degrees. My body was heavily protected by my action-man clothing, and I was still sweating with the exertion of climbing but my face, the only exposed part of me, felt like a block of ice.

"Why am I doing this?" I thought. "Why isn't it Mark or Yvette?"

I shouted to Stephen about the wind.

"What is it that makes you want to spend your life in appalling conditions like this?"

He laughed.

"I suppose the truth is — I like it. Pitting your mind against a problem, working at it — and winning. It's the best thing in life — for me anyway."

At that moment I wouldn't have minded pitting my mind against the problem of pressing two pieces of sticky-backed plastic together in a nice

Action Man: Stephen shows how it is done.

The helicopter flew through the low cloud to land us in a winter wonderland of sunlit snowy peaks against a clear blue sky. There was no flat area so we didn't actually land, but hovered with one ski resting against the slope while we piled out with all our equipment.

Stephen set to work roping us together to begin the long slow trudge to the ice wall. Walking up a steep gradient in full climbing gear, knee deep in powdery snow, is fine for about the first twenty paces. Then the physical effort and the altitude begin to tell, and I found I had little breath for conversation.

"Hold the head of your ice axe, and use it like a walking stick," Stephen advised. As the axe is about two feet long and Stephen is six feet three, I wondered how this was going to work. But as I leant into the gradient and thrust the shaft into the deep snow I began to see what he meant.

The skies were clear and the sun beamed down as we began the long trudge to the ice walk. I looked down at the holes my ice axe was making in warm studio, but I dug my ice axe in, and pressed on. It will get better soon, I thought. I was wrong.

When we reached the foot of the ice wall the weather worsened. There were moments when Stephen, although he wasn't six feet away from me, completely disappeared, and then slowly re-emerged looking like a Yeti.

He helped me to put on my crampons and showed me how to dig in my ice-axe.

"The first thing to do is to keep it away from your face," he said. "Those teeth are like razors. Just bang it in to the ice — like that — and pull yourself up. Only move one axe at a time. If the crampons on your boots are well in, and your other axe is firm you have three strongholds which means you can move upwards."

To my amazement it worked. The axe driven into the ice provided a hold safe enough to haul myself up. Kicking in a foothold with the crampons was more difficult.

As Stephen led off up the ice face, Bill showed me some of the finer points.

"Notice how he keeps his foot horizontal," he shouted. "The blade goes straight in and gives him the maximum hold. If you go in at an angle you tend to slip out again." That's a nice reassuring thought, I pondered, as I saw Stephen battling through the snow thirty feet above me.

I wouldn't have believed it possible. But the weather actually got worse as we were half way up the ice wall. My toes, my fingers and my face had lost all their feeling and I was soaking wet. Suddenly I heard myself calling out.

"Stephen Venables — what are you doing to me!"

Perched on the ridge, gathering in the rope in that appalling blizzard, he actually laughed, like someone hearing a joke at a party.

"Go on — you're loving it really," he shouted down the mountain.

After another terrifying, gruelling, freezing fifteen minutes, Stephen took in the last bight of rope, and I was there on the summit of the ice wall.

He gave a great broad grin and stuck out a snow covered mitt to shake.

"Congratulations, Caron. You've done very well."

It was then that the biggest gust of snow on that dreadful day totally enveloped him. He paused, wiped the snow off his glasses and continued: "Because the conditions have not been very good!"

Action girl: That's Caron on the day she scaled new heights!

Good Luck JET

All yours: Caron and Tessa Martin Bird (left) hand Jet over to Anne Mitchell of the Barrow Farm RDA Group.

TUESDAY 23rd May 1989 was a Red Letter Day for Jet! That was when our Dales pony completed his training and was handed over to his new owners, the Barrow Farm Riding for the Disabled Group.

It was the biggest day in Jet's career so far — after all, *he* didn't know it was HRH The Princess Royal riding him off the lunge rein last year. Jet took it in his stride.

"He hasn't put a foot wrong," said Mrs Anne Mitchell, who runs the Barrow Farm RDA Group. "He's already made friends with another pony, Schnapps, and they're happy playing in our field together."

The handover was satisfying for Tessa Martin Bird, too. She's the expert horsewoman who not only trained Jet, but trained his forerunner Rags, our first Blue Peter pony for disabled riders. Tessa has done over a year of hard work with Jet and it seems to have paid off.

Like all Dales, Jet is strong and powerful. The breed used to haul coal wagons around the collieries of North-east England.

"His strength made him a little wilful in the early days," says Tessa, "but he's responded well to a bit of discipline. He's been very receptive to my voice commands, he is an intelligent, quick learner, and I think he'll turn out to be very good with children."

Anne Mitchell agrees. "He shows every sign of being an excellent pony to work with disabled riders." So good luck to Jet. He has some tough horseshoe prints to follow! Our first pony, Rags, gave over 10,000 rides to disabled people during her twelve-year career and won a long-service rosette from the RDA. Let's hope Jet matches her record!

Easy rider: Jet's first passenger, Caroline Dickson.

Thanks a bunch: The children at Barrow Farm RDA.

GREEN PETER

SAVE OUR PLANET!

SAVE our Planet! That is the message ringing out loud and clear from the children of Britain! And it is the message that has been ringing round our ears, from thousands of letters, ideas, drawings and poems that have bombarded the Blue Peter office since we launched the new Green Blue Peter Badge.

Like all great ideas, it was an incredibly simple one. One afternoon, the production team was planning items for the next few months of programmes. We had been discussing conservation and a film report we were researching about the seal virus in the North Sea. We realised that besides the seals, there are hundreds of different things to do with the environment and our surroundings that people would like to hear about on Blue Peter. "What we need," somebody said, "is some way of focussing, or marking, this huge interest the viewers have got." There was silence.

"Why don't we have a badge, a *GREEN* Blue Peter Badge." The speaker was Nick Heathcote, one of the producers, and one of the most experienced film-makers in the BBC Children's Programmes Department.

As soon as Nick said it, everyone knew that his was a brilliant idea. We knew very well how popular our badges — Competition, Blue, Silver and Gold — are, and we realised that a new badge, combining care for our surroundings with the fame of Blue Peter badges would probably be pretty popular. We did not imagine *how* popular.

We introduced the new badge on the day that we showed a film report about how the children of two Devon villages were helping to preserve their own surroundings. They live near a valley which has the little River Wolf running through it. It is an area, like most of Devon and Cornwall, which gets very short of water, especially in long, hot summers. The South West Water Authority is turning the valley into a giant reservoir which will greatly ease the water problems in the area. That will be good for everyone, but there is a bad part, too. Making the reservoir means flooding the beautiful valley, which will be underwater forever. Valuable and rare ecosystems of plants, animals and insects will

We've got a badge for YOU (above) and (below) one of our first winners at work in Devon.

VE THE EARTH'S

STOP C.f.Cs OK

ok ✓ X

STOP CFCS

BAN CFCS

C.F.C Free

Scor

CfCs CfCs Ban CfCs. Stor

CfCs Ban CfCs. Stop CfCs. Ban CfCs. Stor

C.f.C Free

ONE LAYER

ALL IT IS THE ONLY OTECTION WE'VE GOT!

Me

Mam

Tree

NY WASTE

ACID RAIN

DESTRUCTION

WHO'LL SAVE THE EARTH NOW???

Dear Mark Caron + Yvette,
I am sending a picture of me when I planting a tree for Sutton We did it in Oaks park. were lots of children there hope you like it and t picture I have drawn.
lots of love from
Suzie
Age

Dear Blue Peter,
We are making a conservation garden at school. In the garden we are having a marsh, pond, rockery, meadow, trees, and a hedgerow. Each group has an area to study and a mascot. I have got the pond area to study and my mascot is Tommy Tadpole.
Also, pollution has caught my attention. I have written to our area MP and Mr Kinnock explaining my concern. I have also drawn a poster.
Please could you send me a green
Blue Peter Badge

Dear Blue Peter,
I am li and concerned about the way the world especially pollution.
I recently went to wales adventure holiday the scenery and weather was beautiful Soon as I went to the beach Shocked at the amount of there was lying around come off the passing ship to clean up some of it but beach still looked a mess the could have complaints to Britains coast line
Another thing annoys me is there to fight Christmas wh happened to season of go I love an I have to

Ozone friendly youngs

Ozone friendly pupils... Tommy Tossoun, Richard Tecson, Ewan Allden, Steven Allso Monir Gailani, and Merk Callera, working for a better future

Dear Blue Peter,
HOW AB
STICKER FOR Cars i
in keeping our envir
which could be awa
to change would I
have not got my p
them?!! I did a
and I found out that these stations have unleaded petrol, Elf: Hill Lane roundabout, Upper Shirley. BP: Burgess road, Southampton. ESSO: chickenhall service Sta

A TEAM of environmentally aware Grahame Park pupils are fighting to save the ozone layer.
Seven of the third year pupils of Grahame Park Junior School, aged between nine and ten, are spending their free time working for a better and safer future.
The ozone friendly boys have made badges and posters to encourage others to make the same move. They are also fund-raising for Friends of the Earth and persuading mum and dad to make the same move.
School head David Woolacott said the youngsters became aware of the problem during lessons and general reading.

"They deci were worried to do some produced bad other children things," said N

The pupils about £100 gathered £53 i

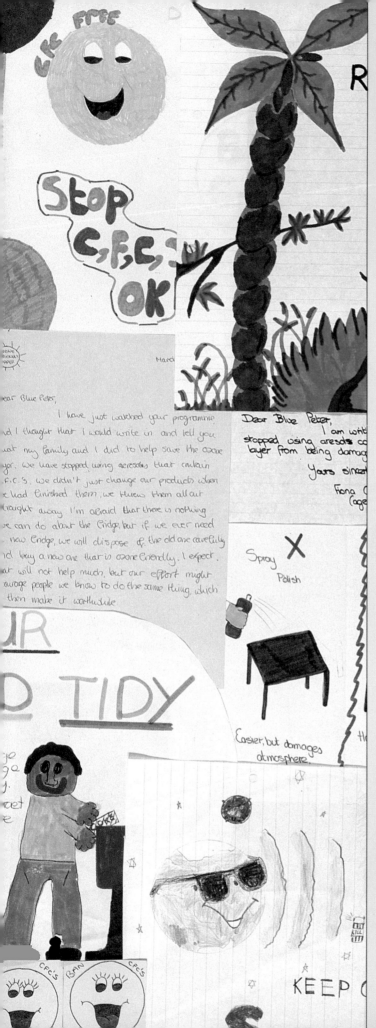

be swept away. Ancient farmland and farm buildings like timbered barns are being destroyed and drowned. It is a high price to pay, but one which is necessary to make sure people and animals have enough water.

The children of Ashwater primary school and Boasley Cross primary school were doing something to preserve their valley. Some were digging up small areas of ground, transplanting wildflowers about to be drowned to their school wildlife garden. And others were recording in pictures and photographs, and by measurements, exactly what the old farm buildings looked like, how they were built and what they were used for. That way, future generations will be able to share the knowledge, and it will not be lost forever.

It made a fascinating film, and when it ended, we explained about the new Green Blue Peter Badge, and what it is for. "We want to hear from *you*," we said. "We want to know what you are doing and what you think about what is happening to our countryside, to our towns and cities, to our planet. We want to know what you think should be done."

And (this is the really great thing about Blue Peter) people started telling us, and haven't stopped yet!

Decorating these pages are just a very few of the tens of thousands of letters we have received. People write and tell us what is happening at their school, or in their cub or brownie pack, what they are doing where they live, what they think the biggest problems are, what kind of pollution annoys or worries them the most . . . just about everything! Reading these letters leaves us in no doubt about something we suspected all along — that the children and young people of this country have been far more aware and worried about the threats to the environment than most adults, and that this is one issue in which children really *can* make a difference. That is quite something, and very important. It is not often that the voices and opinions of children will make governments or big businesses change their minds, or the way they do things. But that is what is happening on pollution and the environment.

We have had masses of letters saying: "I've persuaded my mum to switch to unleaded petrol . . .", or "I told all my uncles and aunts about the dangers of CFC's in aerosols . . ." or "I've joined my local wildlife group . . ."

What are the things people write about most? Well, there is every type of pollution, there is the problem of the destruction of habitats either directly, like chopping down forests, or indirectly, by spewing chemicals into the atmosphere, there is the need to save rare animals and plants. Probably the two most popular things that people write about are at the two ends of the spectrum — one is local to where we live, the other is global and affects the entire world.

The first is litter. This gets people really steamed up, whether they live in the middle of Middlesbrough or out in the Malvern Hills. They

'Operation Eyesore' at Green Wrythe School. Caron joined the dig to transform a wasteland into a wildlife sanctuary.

The next battle in the war to save the ozone layer will be over fridges. We must insist on the fridges we buy not containing CFCs in the cooling elements. So if your family is going to buy a fridge, make sure everyone knows you can buy a fridge without CFCs!

Caron has done her bit to save the ozone layer by abandoning one of the loves of her life — hairsprays. She still uses them of course, but only the pump-action type, not the CFC aerosols. And since she was using about a can a week just by herself, that must have preserved some of the ozone layer!

In the months and years ahead, we hope Blue Peter will continue to report on what can be done to safeguard the world for the future. If we don't, please write and tell us to do it! After all, it is your world, it is the world that you will grow up and live in. What each one of us does now can make a difference to the problems we will face in twenty or thirty years' time. And if you have been meaning to write to us to let us know what you think about pollution, or litter, or the greenhouse effect, or to tell us what your youth club has been doing to improve your local surroundings . . . then do it.

think there is absolutely no excuse for it, it is lazy, should be punished more severely, and makes a mess of where they live.

The second is the ozone layer, the gradual destruction of the layer of gases in the earth's atmosphere that shields us from the harmful rays of the sun. The message about the ozone layer is really getting across to children. We are convinced that most children understand this complicated problem and how it can be solved much better than most adults. If our letters are anything to go by, millions of homes across the country must have completely stopped using aerosol sprays containing chloroflourocarbons, the propellants in the cans that attack the ozone layer. Most aerosols, and nearly all those for general household use — like hairsprays, furniture polish and air freshner — can now be bought in ozone friendly cans that contain no CFCs. That is a change that has not come about because the people who make sprays decided to do it — it has happened because people who use them have asked for it, demanded it and got it. If it was up to most (not all) of the spray manufacturers, we would all still be using CFC aerosols.

THERE'S A GREEN BLUE PETER BADGE WAITING FOR YOU!

JOHN LESLIE

WELCOME to the newest Blue Peter presenter, John Leslie. He's the seventeenth person to present Blue Peter, and the ninth chap! He's the first Scotsman and at six foot four inches, easily the tallest! Here's all you ever wanted to know about John:

DATA·FILE

BORN:	22nd February 1965
HOME TOWN:	Edinburgh
STARSIGN:	Pisces
BROTHER/SISTER:	One brother — Grant — age 21
SCHOOL:	James Gillespies High
FAVOURITE SUBJECTS:	Music and physical education
HATED SUBJECTS:	Did not have any! Honest.
QUALIFICATIONS:	4 O-Levels, 2 CSEs, Certificate in Musical Instrument Technology.
EARLIEST AMBITION:	To play for Hibernian Football Club.
FIRST ACTING EXPERIENCE:	I appeared in our Church play, The Snow Queen, age 7.
HOBBIES WHEN YOUNGER:	Football and music
PETS WHEN YOUNGER:	Rough collie dog called Glen
FIRST JOB:	Newspaper boy
FAVOURITE COLOUR:	Dark Blue
FAVOURITE FOOD:	Steak Diane and Chinese
LEAST FAVOURITE FOOD:	Seafood

FAVOURITE SPORTS:	Football, tennis, badminton and squash
FAVOURITE BAND:	E.L.O. (past) Aztec Camera (present)
FAVOURITE ALBUM:	Faith, George Michael
FAVOURITE TV SHOW:	Cheers and Brookside
FAVOURITE STAR:	Sean Connery
FAVOURITE CLOTHES:	Smart suits and highland dress
FAVOURITE WAY OF SPENDING SATURDAY:	Watching Hibs F.C. in the afternoon and out with friends for a meal in the evening.
BEST FILM EVER:	Top Gun
CAR:	A silver Audi coupé
MOST WANT TO DO ON BLUE PETER:	Parachute Jump
BAD HABITS:	I am a bad loser
COUNTRY MOST WANT TO VISIT:	Australia, to wrestle with crocodiles!
PEOPLE MOST RESPECT:	Mum and Dad for their never-ending support
AMBITION:	Playing in goal for Scotland.

•1975•

•1986•

•1975•

•1971•

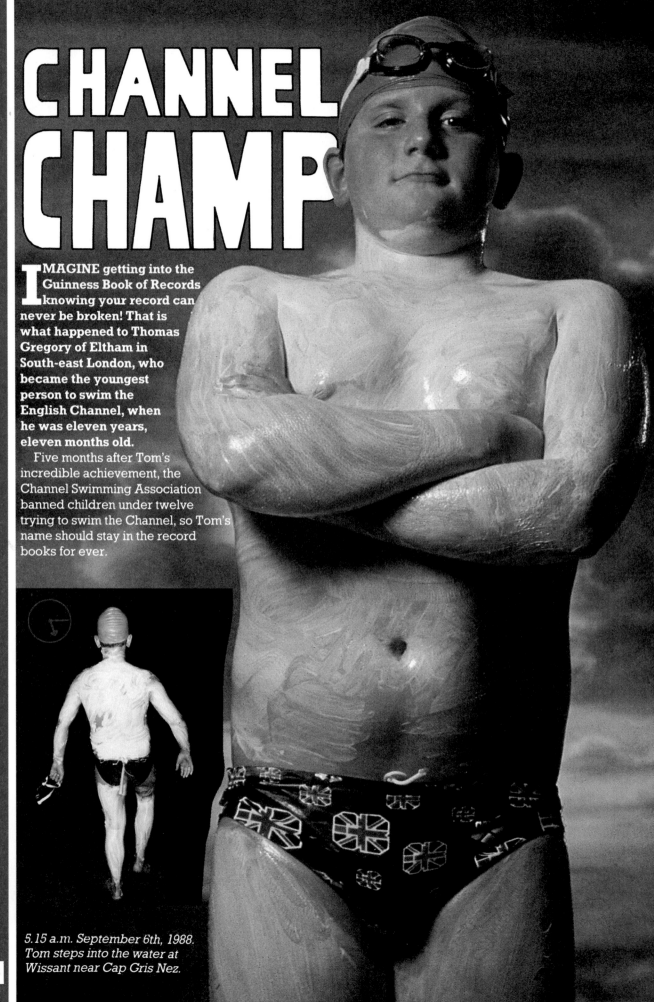

CHANNEL CHAMP

IMAGINE getting into the Guinness Book of Records knowing your record can never be broken! That is what happened to Thomas Gregory of Eltham in South-east London, who became the youngest person to swim the English Channel, when he was eleven years, eleven months old.

Five months after Tom's incredible achievement, the Channel Swimming Association banned children under twelve trying to swim the Channel, so Tom's name should stay in the record books for ever.

5.15 a.m. September 6th, 1988. Tom steps into the water at Wissant near Cap Gris Nez.

If you have ever crossed from England to France by boat, you will know there is an awful lot of sea between our two countries! Even on good days the water always looks grey and uninviting and although the shortest crossing by boat only takes one and half hours, Tom's epic swim took eleven hours 55 minutes. The distance from Wissant in France to Shakespeare Point near Dover amounted to 32 miles — Tom couldn't swim straight across from France, he had to take a zig-zag course because of the tides.

Few adults would take on such a challenge, let alone a child. Why did Tom have a go and how did he train?

It goes without saying Tom likes water! He learned to swim when he was five, at Christchurch School in South-east London. On Fridays he would go to the local baths and amaze everyone by doing elaborate dives before he could swim! Two years later, at Colfe's Prep School, Tom not only got in the swimming, rugby, soccer and cricket teams, he played the cello in the orchestra as well!

But it was joining Eltham training and swimming club that really set Tom on his Channel course. John Bullett, the Club Trainer, took one look at Tom and said: "I'll have him!"

John said afterwards there were three qualities that Tom had that are essential for long distance swimmers — a stocky build, determination and trainability.

Tom started off in 1986 swimming half the length of Lake Windermere — five and a half miles. A year later, he became the youngest person to swim the lake, taking seven hours 50 minutes. This delighted John Bullett, because Lake Windermere is thought of as the qualifier for a Channel crossing. But he didn't want Tom's

school to know of his plan — the teachers had quite a different timetable mapped out and when you think of what Tom packed into the twelve months from September 1987 to September 1988, he deserves a medal for endurance as well as his Gold Blue Peter badge!

Sometimes it was too much even for Tom. One day he packed in training before school, played in a cricket match in the afternoon, acted in the 5.30 performance of Pinnochio and was due to take part in an overnight Swimathon. He had also just taken his Grade IV cello exam. No wonder he fell asleep on the pavement outside the school gates!

So it was quite a relief when school broke up and Tom could go all out for his Channel training. John Bullett thought Tom was in with a chance, so his Mum and Dad organised all the medical reports insisted on by the Channel Swimming

Triumph, land at last! Tom was greeted at Shakespeare Point by his mum and dad and his sister Anna. His coach, John Bullett, also trained the youngest girl swimmer to conquer the Channel.

Association.

And Tom was put on a high energy diet to build him up to withstand the freezing cold sea. This meant eating almost non-stop every day. Porridge with soya and oranges for breakfast, mid-morning snacks of sausages, toast, beans and hamburgers. Jacket potatoes, grilled chicken or fish with vegetables and fruit followed for lunch, with wholemeal bread and biscuits with paté for tea. Supper was more jacket potatoes, steak or liver, or a stew with red kidney beans. And for a late night snack, he would finish up with a tuna omelette and hot chocolate!

On September 5 the weather conditions and the tides were perfect. Tom got ready to leave for France at 10.30 p.m. that night — the big swim was on!

"I wasn't really nervous," he says. "I was just hoping that the moment wouldn't come when I'd have to step into the water!"

Three hours after leaving Dover, Tom — covered head to foot with a thick layer of sheep's wool fat — plunged into the water at 5.15 a.m. for what was to prove a record breaking swim. There was no jellyfish to sting him but his tongue became swollen with the salt from the sea, and once he imagined his tiny escort boat was an oil tanker when it loomed up alongside him.

When he reached the English shore, he was clocking up an astonishing 78 strokes a minute. And just like any other Channel crosser, he went through customs at Folkestone with his passport!

"I don't know if I'd do it again," was Tom's comment when all the excitement had died down. And he has set his heart on his next challenge to take part in a cross-Channel relay team.

He didn't seem all that surprised his photo was in all the newspapers, and when he returned to school, catching up with lessons soon took over from the publicity.

It is good to know that Tom's record will last forever, especially as his brilliant coach, John Bullett, tragically died in January 1989. It comforts all John's admirers and Tom to know his last pupil will always be a world record breaker.

We gave Tom the programme's highest award — a Gold Blue Peter Badge!

RUN·FOR·IT!

Sunday 30th April 1989: Thirty thousand people ran, jogged, walked — even galloped, taking part in the first National Children's Fun Run!

From Aberdeen to Exeter, from Gateshead to Cardiff — and even in West Germany — people joined in. There were fifteen different Fun Run centres in Britain and part of the appeal of the event was that everyone ran on the same day, no matter where they turned up.

It is the first time anyone has organised such a big running event just for children. You have to be 16 to run in marathons — but there was no lower age limit for the Fun Run. The idea came from David Coleman, the famous sports commentator. David works hard for the Sports Aid Foundation, the charity that helps pay for the training of promising sportsmen and women. The S.A.F. split the sponsorship money with the Malcolm Sargent Cancer Fund for Children, a charity which helps children who are less likely to become top athletes, but whose achievements are just as great.

Blue Peter was delighted to launch such a big event. We hope there will be National Children's Fun Runs every year from now on! The applications poured in, and on the big day famous historic and sporting centres all over Britain were being pounded by thousands of trainers and jogging shoes. There were runners at Harewood House near Leeds, round the Aintree Racecourse in

Liverpool, at Burghley House in Lincolnshire, and at the Crystal Palace Athletics Stadium in South London, which is more used to crowds roaring on the Crams and Thompsons of this world that young Fun Runners.

We joined in at the Royal Victoria Park in Netley near Southampton. It is a beautiful spot overlooking Southampton Water, where a hospital for injured soldiers once stood. We set off with nearly a thousand other runners round the wooded pathways of the park. Filming and interviewing en route wasn't the best thing to do while running, especially if you're short of breath! It was just as well it wasn't a race. Mark turned out to be the strongest Blue Peter runner, taking about twenty minutes to cover the three and a half mile course. He strode across the finishing line, clutching his race number which fell off halfway through! John came second, Yvette third, with Caron just behind her. We all seemed surprised we actually made it, especially Caron who had spent the previous month telling anyone who would listen that she wasn't much good at running.

Watch out for next year's event, and if there's a Fun Run happening near your home, why not try and join in?

Fun Runners circling Arthur's seat in Edinburgh.

19

ASLAN THE·GREAT

THE leading character in one of the best children's stories ever written isn't a princess or a spaceman, but the King of Beasts himself — a mighty lion called Aslan. How to bring Aslan to life was the greatest problem that had to be solved when The Chronicles of Narnia was filmed for television. Here's how it happened.

A workshop in West London was where the TV Aslan was born. He was designed and sculpted by Vin Burnham and Vin knew from the start that she

had to convince millions of viewers Aslan was *real*. Whatever happened, he mustn't be comic or like a cartoon character. Even with humans inside him and radio controlled eyes, he had to look as though he had just walked out of the jungle.

C.S. Lewis's marvellous story, The Lion, The Witch And The Wardrobe, is the first of the Narnia Chronicles. It is a tale of the battle between good and evil, and it begins when four children, Peter, Susan, Edmund and Lucy, discover the kingdom of Narnia by walking through a wardrobe!

Narnia is a land of mystical woodland creatures — fawns, dwarves, giants, nymphs and talking animals. Its lord and creator is the great lion, Aslan, who fights a fierce battle with the wicked White Witch, a creature so evil that she has changed Narnia into a land of perpetual winter. For C.S. Lewis, Aslan represented Jesus. And his triumph over the White Witch had a deeper meaning — the death and resurrection of Christ.

It would have ruined the story if Aslan hadn't been convincing. He took Vin and her team three whole months to create and they began with his majestic face. "I made a clay model," said Vin, "but just a bit smaller than life, because it was going to have a thick layer of fur all over it."

The next stage was to take a plaster cast and fill it with soft foam. Then it was ready to be covered with hair. Vin used Yak hair for the mane, and car seat covers for the rest of the head and Aslan's body. The body itself, which began with a skeleton built by Niki Lyons, had to be strong enough for the children to sit on, and hollow enough for two people — Todd and Ailsa — to work the back and front legs. Ailsa manipulated Aslan's mouth, too,

Radio Lion: Controller Tim Rose with designer Vin, Mark, and the beast himself.

making him snarl, smile and roar and even wrinkle his nose.

Aslan's large, gentle eyes were controlled by animatronics. Tim Rose masterminded the mechanics and with a flick of a switch he could get Aslan to look up or down, to left or right, blink and even wink!

Judging by the reactions we saw in the Blue Peter studio, Vin and her team scored ten out of ten. Even people who knew we would never have a real lion walking around Television Centre without a keeper in sight, had the shock of their lives when they bumped into Aslan — especially when his great paws padded towards them and, showing his fearsome teeth, he uttered the gentlest of roars!

I'm sure that like me, the question most people wanted answered was how did Vin make Aslan so realistic?

"By studying the lions at Longleat," she replied. "And getting as close to them as possible." Vin looked at anatomical drawings, too, loads of them. After all, if Aslan was to be convincing, the skeleton of Vin's life-size model had to be like the real thing, otherwise his body would have been the wrong shape.

Some people argue they would rather *not* know about these kind of technical tricks. They say it spoils the magic of the story for them. But I don't agree. C.S. Lewis's adventure is so exciting you just accept that Aslan is real and that he and the children are really flying through the air — even if you know it's all a clever trick. And if it wasn't for the skill of artists like Vin, stories like The Chronicles of Narnia and the Box Of Delights could never be dramatised successfully on TV. Speaking as someone who's seen *inside* Aslan and who knows all the tricks, that is the highest praise I can give. For me, Aslan the character and Aslan the model are both truly great.

And a word with Aslan: Ailsa, the head, says her piece.

HURRY-UP POPPY

Dog meets dog: Poppy, with Amanda, lies next to Bonnie, with Yvette, in the Blue Peter studio.

BLUE Peter has been a friend of Guide Dogs for the Blind for over twenty five years. More recently we met a mongrel called Favour, who is a brilliant member of the Hearing Dogs for the Deaf Association. This year we discovered that dogs have made another leap forward in helping people — Dogs for the Disabled.

Amanda Knapp brought Poppy, her border collie/King Charles spaniel cross to the studio to tell us about it. Amanda is severely disabled and confined to a wheelchair. Poppy is a poppet of a dog, if you'll excuse the expression, but she really is. She has inherited the best in looks from both her mother and her father and the best in temperament, too.

"She was run over by a bus and taken to a dogs' home. That's where Dogs for the Disabled found her," Amanda explained.

There was a rattle at the door we had set up in the studio, and newsboy Mark pushed the paper through the letter box.

"Fetch the paper, Poppy," commanded Amanda. Poppy shot across the room, picked up the paper and returned to Amanda's side, offering it to her.

Dogs for the Disabled is only three years old. It was set up by Frances Hay, who is disabled herself. She had a dog called Kim and Frances discovered that he could be very helpful by bringing her things and picking up articles from the floor which had been dropped and which Frances couldn't reach.

"If Kim can do this for me — what would a properly trained dog be able to do for a disabled person?" she wondered. Thus Dogs for the Disabled was born.

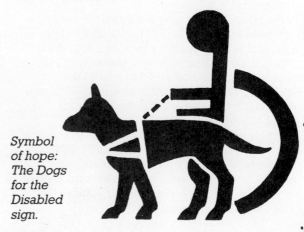

Symbol of hope: The Dogs for the Disabled sign.

Frances started the organisation on a shoe-string, and things were very hard at the beginning. But she had an enormous success with her very first dog, a German shepherd called Rani.

Rani was puppy walked for a year just like a Guide Dog for the Blind. Then she went for a year's intensive training at the Dogs for Disabled headquarters in Warwickshire. When she had completed her course she was placed with an elderly disabled lady called Gladys Rainbow and they got on very well together. Companionship, as I could see from the relationship between Amanda and Poppy, is a very important part of the scheme for both the dog and the disabled person.

One day the old lady had a massive stroke, the condition that completely paralyses one side of the afflicted person. The lady lay on the floor totally helpless and unable to move. Rani rushed up to her mistress, realised at once that she was very ill, and then dashed off to find the cordless telephone. He brought the phone to the lady's side, and she was able to dial 999.

When the doorbell rang announcing the ambulancemen's arrival, Rani completed his brilliant day by opening the door to let them in!

There is no doubt that without Rani's intervention the old lady would have died. The number one dog had proved that Dogs for the Disabled was a success.

Amanda showed me the day to day things that Poppy did for her. Bringing the cordless telephone to her when it rang. Pulling the cord to switch on the light, picking up her pen when she had dropped it, fetching the post and bringing all manner of things to her side, sometimes on command and sometimes off her own bat.

"There's just one thing I'd like to ask," I said. "With you being confined to a wheelchair, what do you do about . . . I mean, what happens when Poppy wants to spend a penny?"

"Easy," said Amanda. "Poppy. Hurry Up!" Quick as a flash, Poppy leapt on the sofa, pushed up the sash window and, with a lion's leap, disappeared from view. She must have had a shock when she discovered that instead of being in her own garden she was in a corner of the Blue Peter Studio, but that's show business!

Poppy and Rani have shown that Dogs for the Disabled is now following the great tradition which began with Guide Dogs for the Blind.

They have proved that when dogs are called man's best friend, it doesn't just mean as companions and pets, but as friends who, when the crunch comes, can even save your life.

ALL TIED UP!

Going to a party and dying to be different? Make one of these designer ties to match your outfit! They're cheap, colourful and cardboard so they're light to wear and they make great presents.

BOW TIES

1. All you need is some stiff cardboard and some trimmings. Begin by laying a ruler on a piece of card and draw down both sides (a).

Draw two more lines (b).

3. To make the bow shape, draw from the corner to the centre line. When you have marked all four, you will see the shape of your tie on the card. Cut it out, and it's ready to decorate.

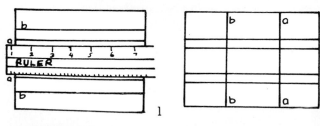

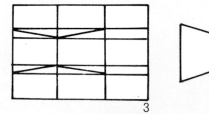

2. Decide how long you want your tie to be and draw a line across the card (a).

Measure the centre of your tie and draw another line across the card (b).

4. You can cover your tie with sticky-backed plastic, or use paints or felt tipped pens.

To fix the elastic, make two holes near the centre. Be careful doing this bit.

5. Use a length of elastic that's long enough to go round your neck comfortably plus a bit extra to tie a bow. Thread it through the holes and tie the bow, so that you can stretch the elastic enough to get it over your head.

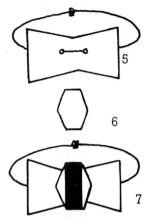

6. To hide the holes, cut out a cardboard "knot" shape and cover it with a piece of sticky-backed plastic.

7. To fix it, hold it in place on the tie and wrap a piece of sticky-backed plastic round to the back and press down firmly.
If you are painting your tie, glue the knot firmly in place and you'll get a very similar effect.

LONG TIES

1. Draw a tie shape on a piece of card, complete with knot. You can use the length of a ruler as a guide.
Start by drawing an oblong then mark the knot (a) and rule straight lines from the corners to the knot to make sure that the finished tie will look neat and symmetrical (b).

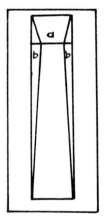

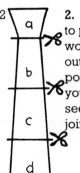

2. When you cut the tie out you need to put some joints in it so that it wobbles and doesn't stick straight out and catch in the custard or poke in your partner's face when you're dancing. Three sections seem about right and making the joints is easy.

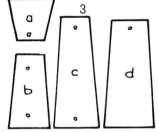

3. Cover the pieces of card with sticky-backed plastic and make holes in the bottom of each piece.

4. The joints are ordinary paper clips — you can choose coloured ones to match the tie — and brass paper fasteners. Push the fasteners through the holes and through the clips and open them out. This not only makes a secure joint but a very good decoration too.

5. When you've fixed all the pieces, your tie will have an excellent wobble to it. And if you cover the backs of the paper fasteners with extra bits of sticky-backed plastic, the ends won't catch in your clothes.

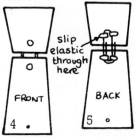

To fix a length of elastic to the tie you don't need to make any holes, just slip the elastic through the paper clip behind the knot.

You can make all kinds of ties in a whole variety of colours using this technique. Your own designer ties at a fraction of the cost in the shops!

PULLING POWER

Tug of war is not a sport that fires the imagination. Two teams pulling on a length of rope until a red marker in the middle goes over the line. I ask you, who needs flair for that? Where are the nicely-judged skills that can turn the fortunes of the game? I'll tell you. After I had spent the day with Gillian Andrew and the England ladies team, I was shouting my head off with enthusiasm.

Gillian, who on first acquaintance seems to have all the fire of a secretary of a ladies' sewing circle, is the one that got us going.

Caron and I had gone to Kirton-in-Lindsey, near Scunthorpe, to meet Gillian and the England ladies team which won a gold medal in Japan last year.

Gillian explained the rudiments of the game that goes back 3,000 years to the Neolithic flint miners of Norfolk. The ancient Egyptians, it is claimed, were tugging a rope thousands of years before that. It became an Olympic sport in 1900 and the first Ladies World Championships were held in 1986.

"You've got to dig your feet in and push off your toes," Gillian said. "And lean right back with your body long. Above all, you've got to be fit. Physically fit, mentally fit and rope fit."

The team's fitness is supervised by Andy Horne, an Army physical training instructor.

After thirty minutes of non-stop press-ups, pull-ups and tearing from one side of the gym to the other with Andy shouting "Move it, Yvette" and "You're idle, Caron," we were physically exhausted and mentally shattered. And we hadn't even seen a rope.

Soft, lady-like hands are not an advantage when pulling on a hemp rope, so Gillian generously squirted revolting, gungy grease on to our palms

That's the way to do it! Gillian shows me how.

to help us to get a grip without taking the skin off our hands.

We lined up along the rope, which I learned to flick up into my hands with a deft kick from the right foot. But there was something missing.

"Where's the opposing team?" asked Caron.

"There it is — all 300 kilos of it," said Gillian, pointing to an oil drum filled with concrete. We would have won when we had lifted it off the ground and winched it up into the trees.

"Right now. Get your hands close to your body," called Gillian.

"Take the strain . . . Pull!"

At first we seemed to be getting nowhere. The oil drum, smugly defiant, stared back from the middle of the field. Then it wobbled, and slowly began to inch into space.

"Well done, girls, we've beaten the concrete."

I collapsed, exhausted, to the floor.

"Get off the floor, flower, you're all right," said the uncompromising Gillian.

The next round was against flesh and blood. The England team, who mostly came from nearby Brigg had challenged another all ladies team from

Caron takes the strain (left) and I feel the pain (below)! Did I really look like that?

'Boring? Not on your life'

Ulceby. Gillian said that Caron and I had to pull for opposite teams so that no one had an unfair advantage. I realised that what she really meant was that neither team should have an unfair disadvantage!

"What do I have to do this time," asked Caron.

"Same as last time — but better," said Gillian.

Caron had stayed with the England team while I joined the visitors.

When we flicked the rope up into our hands something came over me. Whether it was because Caron had joined the opposite team, or whether it was because I was now on the "B" side, I don't know. But I was absolutely determined that when the whistle blew that red marker was going to be on our side.

"Take the strain — Pull!"

I dug my boots in the slippery earth and heaved with all my might.

I heard myself shouting, "Pull it — Pull it" like some demented fan on the touchline — but I was in the thick of it.

No one moved for what seemed like hours. The Guinness Book of Records lists the record duration for a pull as three hours and fifty-one seconds. We had been going for about two minutes and I felt near to the point of exhaustion. This shrill voice kept coming out of my body "come on, come on, pull" it kept saying. I did. I shouted and I heaved. And then I felt that delicious moment, when you know you've gained the advantage.

Pull! Pull! Pull!

The whistle shrilled. We'd won. We'd beaten the England team!

Who said this was a boring game? Not on your life!

Ugh! Our hands were covered in gunge.

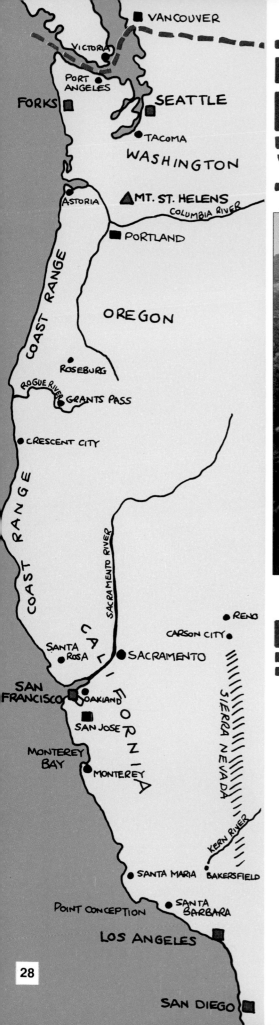

Hi, ya'all! Caron and Yvette in front of the Hollywood sign.

WE saw plenty of bright lights and big cities on our 1988 Summer Expedition to the West Coast of America. But we began our journey cold and wet in what seemed like the middle of nowhere!

We were in the Olympic Peninsula, the top left-hand bit of Washington State, which is the top left-hand bit of the USA. Somehow we thought everywhere in America would be dry and hot in July but in the Olympic Peninsula it seems it rains nearly every day. "Just like home!" we all said, and wondered why we hadn't brought our anoraks. The very first bit of filming we did was in the Hoh rain forest — the only rain forest in North America. It was an enchanting world of mosses and enormous trees, with a forest floor so springy you felt you could trampoline on it!

★   ★   ★

The little town of Forks was our base for filming in the Peninsula. It is a loggers and lumberjacks town, and on America's birthday — the 4th of July — they all came down from the hills to take part in the annual parade. The small-town side of America was something new to us, not the kind of thing we'd expected. There was nothing *Dallas* or *Miami Vice*-like about the children of the local high school band, proudly marching up their town's single main street under the American flag.

Everyone made us very welcome and within a couple of days of arriving in the country, we realised that America is too general a name to describe this vast country. The America we saw during our month of filming has thousands of different faces, from the simple pride of Forks on Independence Day, to the energy and wealth of cities like Los Angeles.

★   ★   ★

One of the most beautiful places we visited on our West Coast tour was San Francisco, the city on the bay, the city of cablecars and rolling hills. If there is a city in a more dramatic position, bordered by water on three sides, we have yet to find it. Perhaps its beauty is what attracts many of its population. As we found on speaking to many people, they love their home, even though it stands a considerable chance of being destroyed or badly damaged in an earthquake. Our base in the city was the only building to survive the last big 'quake in 1906 — the Fairmont Hotel. From its roof the city fathers planned the rebuilding of their city and, in typical American fashion, the city that grew up after the disaster was stronger and bigger than the one destroyed.

★   ★   ★

It was in the Bay area that we learned about the American summer game, baseball. The Oakland Athletics, A's for short, were our hosts and we visited them at their pitch or ballpark, as the Americans call it. We had a batting lesson from René Latchmere, one of America's top coaches.

Log rolling at Forks' Timber Festival — we lasted about one second each!

"That's it, Caron. Hit the ball out past the shortstop. Way to go, Yvette, we'll have you lead off for the A's tonight when we zip the Blue Jays."

Unfortunately it was the A's themselves who got zipped that night, losing one to nothing. And we found the activity in the stands as interesting as the game itself — non-stop food and drink vendors, quizzes and trivia over the huge electronic scoreboard, instant TV replays of exciting moments, a happy crowd with lots and lots of women and children. It was a far cry from a

Dig the gear? Us in real baseball uniforms at the Oakland A's.

29

Look what we bought at Venice Beach!

grey Saturday at a British soccer match.

Before long we had to drag ourselves away from the glories of San Francisco (and its shops) and try the Great Outdoors again. Yvette went white-water rafting down the Kern River in California. She thought she'd seen rapids earlier in the year in North Wales, but they were trickles compared to experiences like White Maiden's Walkway and Dead Man's Curve! Mind you, since the temperature was around 100° Fahrenheit, it was just as well she could rely on an icy ducking every few minutes.

Meanwhile, Caron prepared for one of the greatest adventures of all. It took place with Chuck Nicklin, a world famous underwater photographer. He took Caron out on his diving boat, the Mystique, off the shores of San Diego, and spreading handfuls of a loathsome-looking mixture called chum (bits of cut up fish), he soon attracted a drown of the streamlined eating machines of the deep — sharks!

Sharks! Everywhere! Fortunately, not the Great Whites of *Jaws* fame, but still pretty fearsome terrors — up to three metres long. And they certainly looked frightening when Caron got close to them, diving in Chuck's shark cage with his son, Terry. The sharks criss-crossed the water around the cage and whenever they got too close, Terry just biffed them on the nose to make them go away. This unforgettable dive ended with a

swim through the open water back to the Mystique, past dozens of circling sharks.

The most famous creature we met wasn't a shark, but a bear! If we tell you he's from Jellystone Park, you can probably guess he's not a real one, but Yogi, a star of hundreds of cartoons. We went to the studios in Hollywood where they record the voices for the cartoons and were amazed to find one chubby, middle-aged man acting nearly all the characters. One second he would speak in his own deep, dark-brown voice, the next he would be Boo-Boo, or Scooby-Doo. This was Don Messick, one of cartoon-land's leading voice actors, who you would never recognise in the street. Bet he's turned a few heads by slipping into one of his famous voices! Yvette tried being Yogi Bear's voice — they were looking for a new actor to do that job, but didn't pick Yvette! Caron tried the drawl of Deputy Dawg, and sounded pretty convincing!

★   ★   ★

After our Expedition to the Soviet Union in 1987, we wanted to go somewhere completely different in 1988, and we couldn't think of anywhere better than tho United States. It *is* different of course, the colour and life of the cities, the dynamic new skyscrapers, the variety of shops and restaurants — there are none of these things in the Soviet Union. But what the countries do have in common is size, and that means they both have many, many different types of peoples, who live in different ways with different outlooks. In both countries we got a very friendly welcome from ordinary people. That's probably taught us that, superpowers or not, human beings are pretty much the same, and very nice to be with, wherever you go.

Before we went, Yvette always said that America was the country she most wanted to visit. Now she's seen the West Coast, would she go back? You bet, man! Stay cool!

Caron (in the white flippers) meets Jaws (in the grey suit!).

What a swell place! Yvette takes the plunge and goes white-water rafting.

★   ★   ★

31

CRIME WATCH

HERE were dark doings in Plummers Plain last August. While Caron and Yvette were exploring the USA and I was acting in Billy Liar, thieves broke into the house of a great friend of Blue Peter's — Edith Menezes, who with her husband Jerry, looks after Willow and our tortoise George.

As if having their house burgled wasn't a big enough shock, there was a worse one in store for Edith and Jerry. The thieves had made their getaway via the back of the house, and through the big walk-in wire netting pen Edith had specially built for George, so that he could roam around the soft, Sussex grass with no fears of wandering off into a remote corner of the vast garden or the fields beyond.

Freedom with security was Edith's plan and with a neat wooden box for shelter when the sun was too hot, or the wind too cold, a dish of water and a constant supply of buttercups and fresh lettuce, what more could a tortoise want?

The trouble was, that the bungling burglars left the door of the enclosure wide open. There was no sign of George, so he'd either found the lure of the wide open spaces too strong, and gone exploring, or — horrible thought — he'd been kidnapped. With tortoises fetching as much as £500 each, that was a distinct possibility, and the chances were that we, plus eight million Blue Peter viewers, would never see George again!

By the time Blue Peter returned in September, Edith had been searching for George for four whole weeks. Groups of friends had combed the garden, looking under every plant and bush, but there wasn't a sign of George. There was nothing for it. On our first programme back, we had to announce the sad news that he'd vanished. We even showed a flashback of the highlights of George's

The scene of the crime! George's grand pen in Edith's back garden. The burglars left the door open when they made their getaway with their loot from the house.

"With tortoises fetching £500 each would we ever see George again . . .?"

six years on Blue Peter, so certain we were that he'd gone forever.

But we'd reckoned without Super Sleuth Tod! The day after we'd told viewers about George's disappearance, Tod, a Jack Russell, was out for a walk with his mistress Mrs Arbuthnot. They were near some woods about half a mile away from Edith's garden when Tod leapt into a ditch. Mrs Arbuthnot didn't think that was strange, because Tod's always sniffing out hedgehogs. When she went to investigate, the last thing she expected to see was a tortoise! And because she'd watched Blue Peter the previous day, she knew it must be George.

So thanks to Tod, George was saved from a grisly fate. After six years of hibernating in a snug, straw-filled box, it's unlikely he'd have survived the winter out of doors, and he could well have been attacked by foxes.

A special welcome for George when he returned to Blue Peter after his dramatic disappearance. It was spelt out in carrots with a feast of his favourite sliced cucumber.

We welcomed him back with his name in carrots, a feast of his favourite sliced cucumber, and a lot of admiration. After all, if your legs are only a few centimetres long, we reckon a cross-country journey of half a mile over fields and ditches must be the tortoise equivalent of running a marathon. If George had nine lives like Willow his long distance jog must have used at least eight of them. Can you wonder Edith's put an extra padlock on his pen?

George's rescuer — Tod the Jack Russell terrier.

GERONIMO!

John is roped in to win his Blue Peter Badge

Lazing . . . John takes a break before tackling the huge bridge.

Leaping . . . John jumps for joy (?) from the bridge's parapet.

WHEN people write to Blue Peter saying they want to be presenters, they usually add "I'll try anything!" From now on, our answer will be: "Ah, yes — but would you try bridge swinging?"

That is what John Leslie was asked to try on his very first Blue Peter filming assignment. We had heard about this bizarre new adventure sport and when Stu Thompson invited us to see it, we thought it was an excellent opportunity to give John Leslie a lesson in what being a Blue Peter presenter can involve.

Blue Peter depends on the bravery and nerve of its presenters, but the programme producers always do their best to make sure everything is triple-safe! Bridge Swinging is a growing hobby for mountaineers and rock climbers. If the weather is too grim for climbing, they might jump off a bridge!

John and Mark visited a disused railway bridge in Wales. It stands on huge pillars, forming several arches underneath. The idea of this hair-raising sport is to tie ropes (very firmly!) on to the bridge, loop them under an arch, then jump. The ropes act like a giant pendulum arm, swinging the jumper backwards and forwards under the bridge, until the lack of momentum brings the jumper to a halt, dangling under the arch. Then it is a simple matter of lowering the swinger to the ground.

Stu Thompson showed John and Mark the ropes. They use expensive climbing ropes which cost about £50 each. Each rope could support four or five people on its own. Most swingers wear two or three ropes — John was using four. He inspected the complicated mounting for anchoring the ropes on the bridge and carefully checked his safety harness, which also had a back-up. As in mountaineering, the secret of success is good planning, teamwork and leaving nothing to chance.

As John prepared for his jump, and vertigo-sufferer Mark became more nervous, our special effects cameraman was working out how to get a close-up exciting shot of someone jumping off a bridge. He rigged a camera jutting out from the bridge to catch the actual moment of John's leap to get a close-up picture of his face while in mid-air. But using that camera would depend on John's willingness to jump *twice* — once for the main camera, once for the special effects.

He is a plucky lad, that Leslie. He stuck on his helmet, climbed out on to the narrow ledge on the other side of the bridge wall and prepared to leap.

"It's not too late," said Mark. "You can still change your mind." John didn't hesitate. "When the going gets tough, the tough get going," he said, and with a yell he was gone, leaping into thin air. He fell away from the bridge for a second, before the ropes caught his weight and swung him back and up under the bridge. Up and down he soared, steadily slowing down.

Mark and Stu were there to lower him the last few inches to the ground. "It was brilliant, fantastic!" yelled the excited John. "Would you do it again?" asked Mark. John thought for some time. "No," he replied with finality. "But what about a cup of tea?"

John got his cup of tea, but first Mark gave him his Blue Peter badge. "I think you've earned this," said Mark. He certainly had!

With the right equipment and expert help, bridge swinging is a safe activity. People under 18 should *not* attempt it. You must have the right equipment, which is expensive. You must have experienced experts with you. You must have written permission from the owner of the bridge.

Swinging . . . John almost at the end of his tether.

PREHISTORIC *flight*

How long is it since a brontosaurus was glimpsed in the valleys of South Wales, its long neck snaking into the topmost branches of the trees. A million years ago? One hundred and fifty million years ago? Longer ago than that?

No. It was last February, on the M4 as a matter of fact. It caused quite a stir as well. After all, it's not every day that you check your driving mirror and flash your right hand indicator to overtake a brontosaurus.

To be perfectly truthful there were two of them. They were both strapped on to a low-loader on a windy day, and the driver was worried that they were going to blow off. That might have caused a few problems for motorists.

"Well I was just pulling over to avoid a brontosaurus lying in the middle of the road, officer."

"A brontosaurus, was it sir? Would you mind breathing into this bag?"

The brontosauruses — or should it be brontosauri? — were only two-thirds the size of a normal brontosaurus, and they would only just go under the motorway bridges. So if any *real* ones are fancying a stroll down the M4, I suggest they look for an alternative route, because a bang on the head when it's that size must be a very painful experience.

The ones I was with had been made of fibreglass in Scunthorpe, which sounds an unlikely story I know. A man called Derek Cotton made them. He makes all kinds of prehistoric animals and sends them all over the world. It's true. He sent the last lot all the way to Malaysia, and he has sent some to America as well.

I was driving with them all the way from Scunthorpe to Dan-Yr-Ogof in South Wales. When I say I was driving with them I mean I was in the cab with Richard, the driver. The brontosaurus was following on behind. And his mate, the other brontosaurus was following on behind *him*.

The really difficult bit didn't start until we got to Dan-Yr-Ogof, and I don't mean pronouncing the name either. The theme park where the brontosauri were going to live was half way up a mountain.

It's a good job somebody thought about laying on a helicopter, because I didn't fancy lugging half a ton of fibreglass brontosaurus up a mountain path. Doing "sit and stay" with a prehistoric monster might look eccentric.

Alan, the helicopter pilot, saw no problems. The wind had dropped and the sun was shining. It was a lovely day for flying a couple of brontosauri up a mountain. A few straps were thrown round

BrontoSOARus! A prehistoric beast takes to the air (far left).

Road runners: Our giants set off for South Wales.

That's me down there (bottom) with Richard the driver.

the belly of the number one brontosaurus, the helicopter soared into the air, its dangling strop hooked into the carrying rig, and in no time at all you had one flying brontosaurus.

There was a party of men on the mountainside waiting to grab a set of dangling ropes and pull the swinging beast into position. Alan's crewman leant out of the door and called out instructions to manoeuvre the great herbivore into its final resting place.

"Left a bit — steady — down — down — that's good. Right one foot — steady — steady — down — down — down. That's it. Brontosaurus released!"

Brontosaurus released, indeed.
Back into the wild on a Welsh mountainside.
I wonder what the Flintstones would have said.
"Yabber, dabba, dabba doo!! I've heard of pterodactyls, Barney. But a flying brontosaurus? This is ridiculous!"

BEASTIE BOXES

SICK of being ticked off because you're untidy? With a Beastie Box like these, you'll have a neat solution to a monster problem! Whether you feed them with model cars, puzzles, building bricks, or just use them as a waste paper basket, they'll lurk in the corner of your room waiting to be fed with all your odds and ends. Make them from rubbish and see how useful they'll be.

Cover a grocery box with sticky backed plastic on the *outside* — or paint it, if you prefer. Paint the *inside* a dark colour and make the front outside a dark colour, too.

Make the eyeballs from sticky paper circles. To make the eyes roll, lay one circle down — sticky side up — and lay a piece of cotton on it.

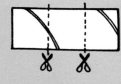

A THE EYE SOCKETS are sections cut from a toilet roll and painted black.

Sandwich the cotton right in the middle of the eye with another sticky white circle. Colour the centre red, with a felt tip pen or paint.

38

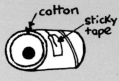

Leave the thread long, because it has to be threaded through the eye socket. Do this with a needle, just like sewing on a button, so that it hangs loose and wobbles in a revolting way. Stick the end down on the toilet roll with sticky tape. Fix the eyes on the box with sticky tape, too.

B THE MOUTH is made from half a plastic pot. Cut the pot in two. One half is just right to make the base for a mouthful of fangs.

C THE FANGS are cut from cardboard. Fix them in place in the mouth with sticky tape.

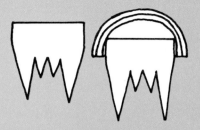

Fix the mouth and fangs on the box with sticky tape. You don't have to do this neatly, because it'll be covered with the Beastie's hair!

1 THE HAIR FRINGES

Wind the wool round a piece of cardboard. The size really doesn't matter, but make it wide enough so that the hair will hang down over the eyes and over the mouth. It doesn't matter if it is too long because you can trim it later. Wind the wool round the card loosely, so that you can slide it down, and make sure that the strands stay neatly side by side and don't overlap.

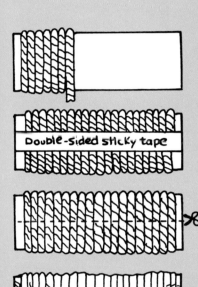

2 When you have a long enough piece, lay the card down and run a strip of double sided tape right along the length and press it down firmly.

3 Cut the wool off the card by snipping down the whole length on the *other* side of the card.

4 Now you have a fringe. If you cut down the length of the double-sided sticky tape, you'll have strips long enough for the moustache and the eyebrows.

5 Peel the backing off the sticky tape and stick the fringes in place. Trim the centre out of the eyebrows so you can see the Beastie glaring, and a bit off the moustache too, so that the fangs show through.

6 Cover the face in exactly the same way, by making more fringes. Use a different colour from the eyebrows and moustache. Start covering the face from the *bottom* and work upwards so that the fringes overlap each other.

7 THE CLAWS

For the final touch cut out some cardboard claws, and cover them with fringes in the same way. Stick the claws to the bottom of the box. You can give them shiny nails by covering the tips with shiny paper.

Finish your Beastie with a fringe stuck around the top edge of the box, for a really neat finish.

Each of the Beasties takes about half a ball of wool — the thickness and colour can be anything you like. No matter what you choose, they'll end up looking really horrible!

Windmill R·I·D·E

HOW many times have you come across a scene like this in the countryside? Not often, I bet! Working windmills, once the most advanced agricultural machinery, are now almost museum pieces.

If it wasn't for a few men like Gerald Thomas, the skills of turning wheat into flour by using wind power would have died out long ago. Most people

A slice of history: Outwood mill in Surrey, Britain's oldest working windmill.

Mastermind: Owner Gerald Thomas, a Master Miller, explains how the windmill works (left).

We are sailing: Yes, that really is me going round on the windmill (right).

buy their flour in paper packets in supermarkets or the corner shop. In the olden days you grew your wheat, or bought if from the farmer, took it to the miller, who ground it into flour in his windmill — and you brought it home by the sackful!

Gerald owns the oldest working windmill in Britain. It is Outwood mill in Surrey, and if you half close your eyes as the mighty sixty-three foot sails whirr through the air, you can easily imagine you are two hundred years back in time, when the miller was one of the most important people in the local community.

You could not have a more simple idea. Each giant sail is a series of shutters, rather like a venetian blind. By adjusting the shutters you can regulate the strength of the wind blowing through them. To start grinding the wheat into flour, you close the shutters up, and as the sails are turned by

the wind, the huge mill stones in the "stonefloor" inside pulverise the wheat to dust. Gerald says in a force four wind his mill produces a hundredweight of flour every hour.

There is a lot of hard work involved. That is why millers always used to be powerful men with the physique of a Frank Bruno or a Geoff Capes. Not only because they had to hump all the sacks of wheat and flour, but because they also had to set and start the sails *and* put the brake on when they wanted them to stop turning. I was puffed out when Gerald got me to lend him a hand with that. The brake was a rope connected to a huge wooden lever inside the mill, and it took all my might even to slow the sails down, let alone stop them!

Just as I was beginning to think being a Blue Peter presenter was far easier than being a miller, Gerald had another torture up his sleeve.

Hang about! The world looks strange when you are upside down.

"You know Mark", he said with a wicked twinkle in his eye, "you can't be a Master Miller like me until you've been round on the sail."

"Oh yes," I replied. "What's that mean?"

"Exactly what I say — you go round on one of the sails."

My face must have been a picture. Me — with my fear of heights — clinging on to a windmill sail as it spun full circle, like the ferris wheel at the Blackpool fun fair!

"I tell you what," said Gerald, "how about if we strap you on?"

I must have been mad. But Gerald made it sound so simple I agreed. With my feet in straps and a safety harness around my waist, I was fixed on to a sail with a special film camera above me — to record my "reactions", said director Alex Leger. I told him I would probably throw up!

As a matter of fact, I didn't. It was incredible to see the view, upside down at the top of the circle — like being upside down at the top of Mount Everest.

But although Gerald and Alex said I was brave, I didn't score top marks for my commentary. All I could come up with was "Oohh — quick!" "Oh — it's incredible!" "Once more — then that's it — Ohhh!"

I could hardly believe that Gerald has done it *without* being strapped on *and* climbed from sail to sail. He is a brave man and certainly deserves his title of Master Miller.

But although riding the sail was a bit of bygone folklore, there is a good chance that windmills may be a familiar sight in Britain in the 21st century. With wind power high up in the energy saving stakes, mills like Gerald's could be a big step forward in the Green campaign — and that can't be bad!

DRESSED TO KILL

This looks very pretty — but it meant death for thousands of birds . . .

ONE hundred years ago thousands of egrets, birds of paradise and herons were slaughtered during their breeding season. Why? To provide feathers for the hats of wealthy, fashionable ladies. "You simply never went out without one, darling." But help was at hand. In 1889 the Royal Society for the Protection of Birds was born.

It was during the breeding season that the bird's plumage was at its most spectacular. The fact that it also meant millions of chicks being orphaned in the next was immaterial to the traders and uninteresting to the wearers.

But not quite every woman in the land was prepared to turn a blind eye to the suffering of birds in the name of high fashion. Two groups of women, living at opposite ends of the country, determined to put an end to this barbaric trade in plumes.

Mrs Margaretta Louisa Lemon of Croydon went to church on Sunday and wrote down the name of every lady she saw wearing a feathered hat. The next day she wrote a letter to each one explaining: "The cruelty of this practice which means the starvation and death of numberless orphans and fledglings . . ."

Two hundred miles further north in Didsbury near Manchester, another anti-plumage group of women was being set up at around the same time. This was led by Mrs Robert S. Williamson and called The Society for the Protection of Birds.

Two years later, these two groups of formidable women, as they were called, got together and set up an office in London for the SPB — the R for Royal was still to come — determined to stop the killing of birds for their plumes once and for all. They masterminded a plan to bring the plight of the birds to everyone's

The spectacular white egret. Its feathers were prized by the rich and fashionable.

The 'formidable ladies' who stopped the slaughter — Mrs Robert S. Williamson (left) and Mrs Margaretta Lemon. Together they saved thousands of birds.

The bird of paradise — nature at her most magnificent. But its brilliant plumage brought death in the breeding season. ▶

Ospreys were wiped out in Britain — hunted to extinction by gamekeepers. But when a breeding pair returned to Scotland the RSPB stepped in. ▼

rooms it grew into the biggest wildlife conservation organisation in Europe. It was given the title Royal in 1904, and today with half a million members, controls 114 large areas of land as nature reserves for birds.

The RSPB now protects birds from egg collectors, pesticides, modern farming methods and the endless march of the towns that every year take over more and more of the countryside which was the breeding ground for our birds.

One of the Society's greatest successes has been the osprey. This glorious fish hawk completely disappeared from Britain for fifty years. It was so brilliant at fishing the trout from the lochs and rivers of Scotland that the gamekeepers hunted it out of existence. Then, miraculously, on a spring day in the mid Fifties, the two birds appeared at Loch Garten in Scotland and began to build a nest. The ospreys had returned to Britain!

Once again the breathtaking aerobatics could be seen as they plunged from the skies to hit the loch in a flurry of spray and carry away a wriggling trout in their talons. The nesting area was declared a sanctuary and a day and night watch by volunteers of the RSPB was mounted on the shores of the loch. But in spite of this the ruthless egg collectors broke through and in 1958 at the dead of night they climbed the osprey's tree and robbed the nest. People were afraid that the osprey would disappear from Britain again, but by another miracle they returned the following spring, and today there are fifty-two pairs of breeding ospreys nesting each year in Scotland.

I joined Roy Dennis of the RSPB at a secret location in Scotland to do a spot of repair work on an osprey's nest. During the winter, while the ospreys were on their migratory trip to Southern Africa, a gale had blown their nest out of the hundred foot-tall Scots pine tree that had been their home.

attention, with schemes like sandwichmen parading outside the fashionable West End shops to proclaim their message.

Finally, in 1931, after more than thirty years of struggle, the Government passed The Importation of Plumage Bill, banning the feathers from birds which would have to be killed to ensure their collection from entering Great Britain. The formidable ladies had won!

This was just the beginning. The Society broadened its aims to include *all* birds and from those humble beginnings in suburban sitting

It wasn't that Roy was afraid that the ospreys wouldn't build their own nest again, but by giving them a head start we could increase their chances of success by giving them more time to lay eggs.

Roy climbed to the top of the tree with a saw and began to create a landing site for the birds while I, like a good osprey, collected the sticks and the moss to build the nest. I was able to re-use a lot of material from the old ruined nest that had been blown to the ground.

Ospreys, I discovered, will use anything that comes to beak or talons to build their huge metre-wide nest. I rescued a piece of wheel trim from the wreckage of the old nest. The osprey had obviously realised it would be useful and carried it back to help bind the nest together.

Great boughs of Scots pine came crashing down from the top of the tree. Roy explained that with their vast wing spans the ospreys need space to land. And the uninterrupted view from their eyrie would enable them to spot other osprey up to ten miles away. This would help them to plot where the best fishing grounds in the neighbourhood were likely to be.

I climbed to the top of the ladder to help Roy assemble the nest and to get an osprey's eye view of the Highlands that was absolutely breathtaking.

I thought for a moment about Mrs Lemon and Mrs Williamson and I felt very proud to be a girl, helping in a very small way the organisation that 'those formidable ladies' had begun, a hundred years ago.

Friends in high places! Caron and Roy repair an osprey's nest — with the aid of a giant crane.

RSPB

ROBIN HOOD

Robin Hood,
Riding through the glen
Robin Hood, Robin Hood,
With his band of men
Feared by the bad
Loved by the good
Robin Hood, Robin Hood, Robin Hood!

Blow me! Robin Hood meets Little John.

DID Robin Hood really exist? If he did, was it really like that? Did he really rob from the rich and give to the poor? Or, as American comedian Mel Brooks says, did he rob from the rich and keep it all himself?

Like most good legends, the Robin Hood story is founded on some true-life fact. There was a nobleman, called Robert Lockesley, who had his lands seized. It is thought he was forced into hiding in the forest. But clothes of Lincoln Green, poaching King John's venison, leading the Sheriff of Nottingham a merry dance, the stories of Friar Tuck, Little John and Much the Miller's Son are all these the result of centuries of exaggeration and wishful thinking?

We sent our very own Little John to Nottingham to investigate. Sherwood Forest is smaller these days, but a massive tree — the Major Oak — does still stand, with timber beams propping up its enormous, spreading branches. Did Robin and Maid Marion whisper sweet nothings to each other under the leaves of this tree? Probably not, since the Robin Hood legends go back eight hundred years, and scientific tests show the tree to be a youngster — no more than six hundred years old!

So off to Nottingham itself. The Sheriff's castle is long gone unfortunately. But the new Robin Hood Centre in Nottingham is a modern attempt to throw some light on the ancient legend, and give tourists something to look at when they come in search of Robin and his Merry Men. The centre is a £1.7 million project which is designed along similar lines to the vastly successful Jorvik Viking Centre in York.

It is a series of tableaux, complete with mysterious compact disc voice-over and sound effects, which take the visitor on an adventure car ride through a recreation of medieval Nottingham. John took the ride with Graham Black, who has tried to make the creation of medieval Nottingham in the twentieth century as realistic as possible. John fled from the Sheriff's men, as thousands of visitors will do, but couldn't really make up his mind about whether Robin Hood really existed, even after visiting the Robin Hood exhibition, which is part of the same attraction. It would be a shame if all the marvellous Robin Hood stories turn out to be a load of thirteenth century bunkum. Fortunately, this is one question the historians and scientists will probably never be able to answer. We'll never know

Low-down on a legend: John and Graham Black underground at the Robin Hood centre.

for sure, so we can go on believing all the old legends. In the meantime, the spirit of Greenwood hangs once again over Nottingham and the wicked and the wrong best beware — Robin Hood might be after them!

A dozen rusty, dusty lorries can never have been a more welcome sight! Caron and a Blue Peter film team found them in Phnom Penh, about to head out of their depot with deliveries to be made all over Kampuchea. They are some of the fifty-seven lorries Blue Peter viewers bought ten years ago for the people of Kampuchea, and they're still working hard as you read this!

They're living proof that Blue Peter Appeals really DO work, and go on working, providing long-term aid, for years and years. That's what we're sure the second Blue Peter Bring & Buy Sale for Kampuchea in 1988 will do, just as the 1979 Appeal did.

Ten years ago, the country was called Cambodia, and the world was learning with horror about the murder and destruction carried out by Pol Pot and his brutal army, the Khmer Rouge. They seized power in 1975 and, when they were overthrown four years later, it was discovered that the Khmer Rouge had killed up to two million of their own countrymen and women. It is hard, even today, to believe that such a tragedy could have happened. But happen it did, as the Khmer Rouge closed off Kampuchea from the outside world, and followed their perverted policies and ideas.

In their topsy-turvy minds everything to do with progress — like electricity,

Still working after all these years — three of the lorries bought by viewers ten years ago.

Avonmore Primary School sent pictures of their Bring & Buy Sale.

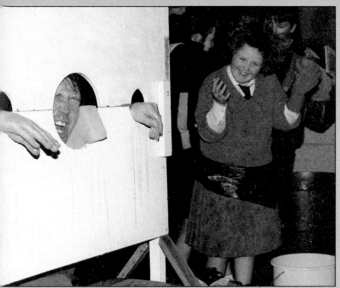

▲

*At Hedworthfield Comprehensive
School pupils paid ten pence
a sponge to soak their teacher.*

Top right:
*The Kompong Chan Ferry —
a lifeline across Kampuchea.
It's ten year refit will be paid for
by your Bring & Buy Sales.*

◄ *All girls together:
Caron makes some
new friends.*

schools, factories — had to be destroyed.
Families were split up, music was
abolished and people were sent to work in
the fields as slaves, where death by hunger
or beating was their probable end.

In 1979, when the truth about
Kampuchea was revealed, Blue Peter
viewers led the world in responding to the disaster. They raised
£3¾ *million* — easily the most money raised by one of our Appeals
— and bought those lorries as well as tools, nets, seeds, 200
irrigation pumps *and* a ferry! A lot of that material — besides the
lorries, Caron came across people repairing roads using our hoes
— is still being used.

Some of it is worn out and, by the autumn of 1988, badly needed
replacing. Unfortunately, in the years since 1979, Kampuchea has
received next to nothing from the rest of the world. Vastly
complicated politics and arguments between super-powers have
kept relief away, and now the Kampucheans live in probably the
poorest country in the world. It is essential that they keep what
little they've got, and so we felt it was up to us to repair the ferry
and the pumps, just as we replace worn out Blue Peter lifeboats
here at home.

We launched the Appeal not only by requesting your help with
the pumps and ferry but also by explaining one of the biggest
threats to the capital, Phnom Penh. The city's water purification
plant keeps breaking down, allowing dirty water to get into the
drinking supply. Pol Pot killed most of the engineers who ran the
plant. Few new materials have been brought in to repair it, nor
have many new engineers been trained. A giant model of the
waterworks in the studio showed the problem. You, we said, have
the power to fix it.

The first Blue Peter Appeal for Kampuchea was the time we
invented the Great Blue Peter Bring & Buy Sale, so we copied the
idea for the second Appeal. Within days thousands of Bring & Buy
Sale kits were being despatched from Oxfam to addresses all over
the country, as well as to Belgium, Holland and British families in
West Germany and Cyprus — all places where Blue Peter is
watched.

The Appeal quickly gathered steam and moved towards the first
target we'd set on the Totaliser of £150,000. That might seem a low

RETURN TO KAMPUCHEA

We held a Bring & Buy Sale in the famous Petticoat Lane Market in the East End of London.

target, but to us, at the time, it seemed like a lot of money to raise for a country that, unlike Ethiopia or Armenia, has not been in the headlines. But thanks to the film reports Caron made in Kampuchea, the sights and sounds of Phnom Penh and the surrounding countryside soon became well-known.

Caron filmed in the rice fields, where she saw how the irrigation pumps could more than double the rice harvest. She saw ancient temples, the signs of a proud, religious civilisation that existed in Kampuchea before the Khmer Rouge, and which showed what a happy and prosperous country Kampuchea was before it became caught up in the wars of South-East Asia over thirty years ago. Caron went to the waterworks in the capital, and met the men who keep it running. She saw the green field where Oxfam hope to build a training school for the engineers of the future. And, unforgettably, she saw the hospital where the beds were full of undernourished children critically ill from diarrhoea, dysentery and other severe illnesses caused by dirty drinking water. Sadly, many of the children Caron filmed are not alive today.

At home, the plight of the Kampuchean people brought an incredible display of generosity, hard work and love from the children of Britain. "We want to show the Kampuchean people they haven't been forgotten" was what we said when we launched the Appeal, and you made those words come true. We sailed past our £150,000 Target after just two weeks, and raised it to *one million pounds*. Fortunately, Blue Peter viewers came up with the goods – over twenty thousand Bring and Buy Sale

Much of Phnom Penh's water is filthy, drawn by hand from pipes that often overflow with sewage.

The water seller (below) is a common sight in the capital.

kits were sent out and soon our map showing where the sales were happening was so crowded, you could hardly stick another pin in anywhere.

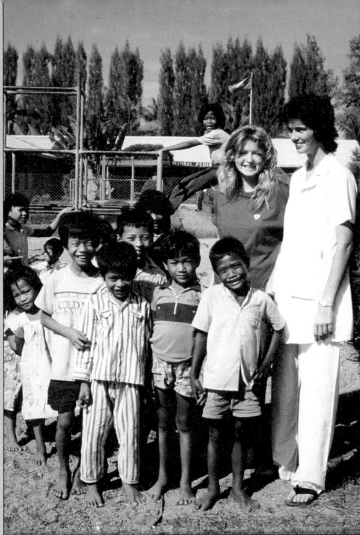

Smiles of recovery at Phnom Penh Children's Hospital. In future, fewer children should be laid low by diarrhoea and dysentery thanks to the clean water you provided.

Summit talks: Caron explains the desperate situation in Kampuchea to Prime Minister Margaret Thatcher.

Our Appeal even came to the notice of the Prime Minister, Mrs Margaret Thatcher. We asked if we could talk to her about Kampuchea, because she's spoken out strongly against allowing Pol Pot, who still has troops in the hills on the border of Kampuchea and Thailand, to return to power. The British Government do not send much aid to Kampuchea though. Pol Pot was removed from power by an invasion from neighbouring Vietnam, and Britain does not agree that the new rulers in Kampuchea are the rightful leaders of the country. Britain has been very involved with other countries like America, France, the Soviet Union and China in trying to work out a peaceful future for Kampuchea, without Pol Pot and without the Vietnamese.

Mrs Thatcher was happy to talk to us, so just before Christmas Caron and a film team went to Number Ten Downing Street. Mrs Thatcher announced that the British Government was going to send more aid — £250,000 — to Kampuchea and said much more would follow once the Vietnamese had left. She also said that she thought there were some people in the Khmer Rouge who would have to be allowed to take a small part in the new, future government in Kampuchea. That was a view which puzzled Bill Yates, the Oxfam expert who filmed in

Kampuchea with Caron. Oxfam's belief is that nothing the Khmer Rouge have ever done has showed that they've changed from the brutal thugs they were ten years ago.

It is clear that Kampuchea still has a long struggle ahead along the road back to the happy, prosperous country she was thirty or forty years ago. Her fate will be decided around the conference tables in capitals far away from Phnom Penh. Let us hope her people are given the chance to live in peace, and are given the tools to do the job of rebuilding their country. They've performed near-miracles with the little they've had since 1979. Now, thanks to the generosity of Blue Peter viewers, they can get the waterworks going again, repair hundreds of irrigation pumps, keep that vital ferry running, and perhaps most important of all, train the mechanics and engineers of tomorrow. They don't need sacks of grain delivered by emergency planes, or loads of blankets — they need the kind of help you've given them, so they can look after themselves. You've helped them on the way, and you've told the happy, confident people, who've been shut off from the world for ten years, that here in Britain there are millions of people who know about them, and who care about them.

Caron's C·l·o·t·h·e·s ompetition

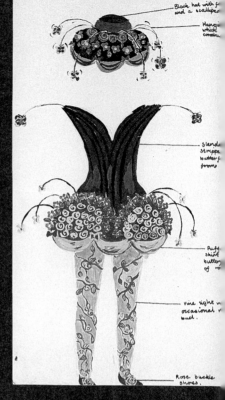

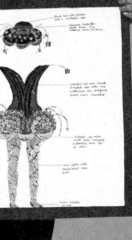

Jasmin comparing her winning entry with the real thing.

69,928 children took up the greatest challenge we've presented in a Blue Peter competition — design a new outfit for the trendiest lady on television, Miss Caron Keating!

And what a winner! Chosen by Caron herself, the work of 11-year-old Jasmin Nealon blazed with ideas, colour and originality. Butterflies delicately fluttered from the hat, bodice and skirt; fluffy yards of pink net billowed from Caron's waist; beautiful pink hand-sewn roses were everywhere, even decorating the hand-painted tights.

The winning entry was chosen on a Monday. The BBC Costume Department had

Dozens of hand-sewn pink roses decorated the skirt . . . ▶

. . . and butterflies fluttered around the hat.

precisely one week to work out how to make it, what to make it of, find the materials and get sewing! The main dress, made out of lush red velvet, didn't take long, but those roses! It was all hands to the needle, as dozens of roses had to be produced to give the effect Jasmin painted in her entry.

Jasmin was watching at a friend's house when her entry was revealed as Caron's favourite. Her father said she almost fell off her chair with surprise! When we checked up, we found Jasmin, who comes from Edinburgh, was no stranger to success in Blue Peter competitions — she won a third prize in our Butterfly Mural competition with a dreamy picture in gentle pastels. It was the butterflies that got her started on the design for Caron's Clothes competition. She began with the way they droop from the hat, then her ballet lessons came in useful for the rest! Look closely, and you'll see the dress resembles a ballerina's tutu!

Caron loved all of it. She loved the hat, she loved the dress, she *particularly* loved the green tights with their roses rambling around them. And with her eye for fashion, and for anything individual, she knew it would look good.

Just how good was a surprise for all of us. When Caron first appeared in the studio wearing Jasmin's dress there were gasps from just about everyone. Tina Waugh, our costume designer, and her colleagues in the BBC costume department did a superb job, working up to the very last minute before we went on air, pinning and fussing to get it looking just right. As you'll agree from these pictures, there's never been an outfit like it. And if Jasmin ever fancies a career as a clothes designer, what better drawing to have in her portfolio — the one that stunned eight million viewers out of a British winter and into a tropical fairyland of butterflies and roses!

S·P·E·C·I·A·L
APPLE SPONGE

Dear Blue Peter,

I am 8 years old and last year I became Diabetic. This means I can't digest sugar or starch without insulin. Did you know there are hundreds of thousands of children Diabetic just like me! So I can't enjoy your lovely recipe's any more. So I am sending you some of the recipe's I like, Maybe you would show them on your programme. I am sure everyone will love them including Me!!!!

Love from

Lucy Carruthers.

LUCY was right! There are an estimated one million people in Britain who are diabetic and eighteen thousand of them are children. This doesn't mean they can't live perfectly normal lives, but they do have to be careful what they eat and, most important of all, they must try not to eat too much food containing sugar.

When Lucy came on Blue Peter she told us she and her Mum had made up all kinds of scrumptious recipes using sugar substitutes, so she hasn't had to give up all her favourite foods. One alternative to sugar is called fructose — a fruit sugar which you will find in most chemists and health food shops. It is more expensive than ordinary sugar, but if it means that people who are diabetic can enjoy

something sweet, it could be worthwhile. There are two trade names — Fruisana and Dietade — and Boots produce a fruit sugar, too, called Fructose Powder.

But even if you use a fruit sugar, the British Diabetic Association say it is important you don't have more than 25 grams or one ounce in any one day, because fructose is no lower in calories than ordinary sugar.

One of Lucy's most mouth-watering recipes was for Apple Sponge, and this is what she demonstrated on the programme with Chef Curry as her assistant. It is very simple to make and inexpensive. Here is what you will need:

1 large apple
A little lemon juice
4 heaped tablespoons of self-raising wholemeal
flour or rice flour
½ heaped teaspoon baking powder
½ heaped teaspoon cinnamon
75 grammes (3 ounces) margarine
2 tablespoons skimmed milk gently heated
2 large eggs
2 level tablespoons of fructose

1 Peel and core the apple and cut into slices. Cover with water and add a little lemon juice. Cook until mushy (about five minutes). Drain and leave to one side.

2 Mix together the flour, cinnamon and baking powder and in a separate bowl, beat the margarine and fructose until it's light and creamy.

3 Separate the egg yolks from the whites, by breaking the eggs one by one into a saucer. Holding a small cup over the yolk, pour the white off into a bowl.

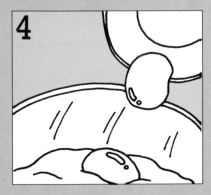

4 Add the two egg yolks to the margarine and fructose mixture and stir well.

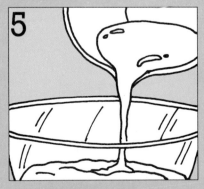

5 Add this to the flour mixture and add the gently heated milk.

Beat the egg whites until they're light and fluffy and stiff enough to stay in the bowl when you

6 hold it upside down! To keep the bowl steady, put a damp dishcloth underneath it. Then gradually fold the egg whites into the mixture, using a metal spoon.

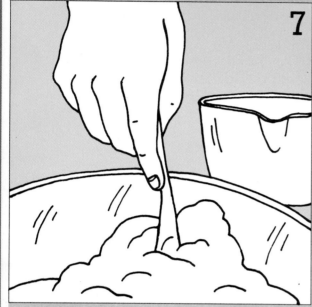

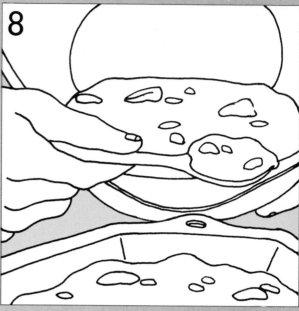

7 **8**

Fold in the drained, cooked apple.

Spoon the mixture into a shallow, greased, ovenproof dish and bake in the oven for 20 minutes, or until your Apple Sponge is golden brown, at 190°C, 375°F or Gas Mark 5.

A good way of testing whether sponge is ready is to push a metal skewer into the middle. If it pulls out clean, with no crumbs on it, the sponge is cooked. Otherwise stick it back in the oven for a few more minutes.

Lucy's Special Apple Sponge was very tasty on its own. But you could always add a dollop of diabetic jam or some extra stewed apple.

We are looking forward to sampling more of Lucy's recipes. Even if you are not diabetic, most people eat too much sugar, so these are a useful alternative.

If you *are* diabetic, and you would like to know more about the special food that is available, you will find details in 'Useful Information' at the end of the book.

THE BABY BEAS

Double Beas: The new Princess Beatrice (above) with her mother, the Duchess of York and the first Princess Beatrice (right) aged three weeks.

WHEN the Duke and Duchess of York announced the name of their baby daughter as Beatrice Mary Elizabeth people were surprised, because Beatrice is not a common name now. But there was a Princess Beatrice once before. She was the great, great, great, great, great aunt of the new Princess Beatrice. She was the youngest child of Queen Victoria and, when she was born 131 years before *our* Princess Bea, Prince Albert announced: "It is a fine child, and a girl!" She was christened Beatrice Mary Victoria Feodore. But because she was the youngest of Queen Victoria's nine children, all her family called her Baby.

To escape from their grand, royal palaces, Queen Victoria and Prince Albert built Osborne House on the Isle of Wight as a holiday home. It is a lovely place and when I filmed there for my Treasure Houses series, I could understand why it became Princess Beatrice's favourite home. She lived there until the very end of her life, and if *you* ever go to the Isle of Wight you can visit Osborne House and the church, close by at Whippingham, that Prince Albert designed.

NOW: *Mark visiting Osborne House today (above).*
THEN: *Osborne in May 1857 with Queen Victoria holding Beatrice surrounded by the rest of the family (left).*

Beatrice the first, aged three (below).

Although Queen Victoria had been quite strict with her other children, Baby was everyone's pet. When she was a little girl, Beatrice wasn't afraid of anyone — not even the Queen herself.

The story goes that, one day, sitting in the royal dining room, Queen Victoria told her she was not allowed any of the rich pudding on the table.

"That's not good for Baby," she said. "But Baby likes it, my dear," replied Beatrice, coolly helping herself!

She was a very observant child. After seeing how her parents spent hours each day working at their writing desks, whenever Beatrice was asked to do something she didn't fancy, she would reply: "I have no time — I must write letters!"

But when the little Princess was only four years old, her father Prince Albert died. Queen Victoria was heartbroken and became sad and gloomy. All five princesses wore black dresses and were expected to be very solemn all the time. Queen Victoria never recovered from Prince Albert's death and Baby was a great comfort to her. All the other princesses married and left home, but the Queen was so afraid her youngest daughter would leave her too, that she tried to stop her growing up. People were forbidden to talk about weddings in front of her, and if she ever went to a party or a ball, she was only allowed to dance with her own brothers.

So poor Beatrice stayed at home, writing letters or reading aloud to her mother, with no friends of her own age, and no freedom to decide anything for herself. People called her The Shy Princess — but when she was twenty-seven years old, everything changed.

Princess Beatrice went to Germany, where her niece was to marry Prince Louis of Battenberg. He had three brothers, and one of them, Henry, or Liko as he was called by the family, fell in love with Bea. Queen Victoria was furious! She refused to allow them to marry and hurried back to Osborne, taking Beatrice with her. She vowed that as long as Beatrice wanted to marry Liko, she wouldn't speak to her. But Princess Bea refused to give in. For a while, Queen Victoria had to write notes to her daughter and pass them across the breakfast table! The Princess who had seemed so shy as a teenager was determined to get her own way.

Bea and her sisters in mourning for their father (left).

The Princess was an accomplished artist. She decorated this poem (right).

To try and persuade the Queen to change her mind, Liko and Beatrice said they would live in England, not Germany, and in the end Queen Victoria agreed to their marriage. But she said she could not stand a huge wedding in London, so it took place in Whippingham Parish Church. No Royal Princess had been married in a Parish Church before, but Beatrice was not sorry. She had been confirmed there, it had a memorial to her father and her mother worshipped there every Sunday she was at Osborne. Later Princess Beatrice gave one of her wedding presents to the Church — a beautiful bible with her name inside.

She and Liko had four children. They called Queen Victoria "Gangan", and she loved them dearly.

But Beatrice only had ten years of happiness with Liko. He was taken ill and died in a country in West Africa where he had gone to fight with the British Army. His body was brought back to England and buried in Whippingham Church. Later Beatrice designed a monument to him. Once more, she became Queen Victoria's constant companion, but five years later, the Queen died, too.

Beatrice succeeded her husband as Governor of the Isle of Wight and she lived there until the Second World War. She died in 1944 aged eighty-seven and she lies beside her husband in the little parish church of Whippingham, where they had been married all those years before.

The new Princess Beatrice will have a very different life. But apart from her name, she already has something else in common with her great, great, great, great, great aunt. They both have places named after them. The baby Princess has a mountain in the Himalayas named after her by two British climbers who conquered the peak. And the first Princess Beatrice had a town in America named after *her*. We showed the local paper on the programme — the headline read "Beatrice: A Great Place to Live". Who knows, perhaps the present Princess Beatrice will visit Beatrice one day!

Mother and daughter: Bea and Victoria in 1879.

Bea and her beloved Liko on their engagement.

GOLDIE'S W·O·N·D·E·R·S

BY THE TIME THIS PHOTO WAS TAKEN, ALL SEVEN OF BONNIE'S BROTHERS AND SISTERS HAD PASSED THEIR GUIDE DOG TESTS WITH FLYING COLOURS. GOLDIE'S SECOND LITTER REALLY IS WONDERFUL! HERE'S HOW IT ALL HAPPENED . . .

WAY back in 1978, a seven-week-old golden retriever puppy joined Blue Peter — on the same day as a brand new presenter called Simon Groom. Goldie came from a litter that had been bred for the Guide Dogs for the Blind Association, but Puppy Walking Manager Derek Freeman, did not think she would quite make the grade as a Guide Dog. That was very lucky for Blue Peter. Goldie was given to us, and in return, the programme made a promise. We said that if Goldie ever had puppies of her own, we would let Guide Dogs have the pick of the litter and choose whichever ones they thought would be suitable for them to train. So each time Goldie was mated, the dog was a Guide Dog stud — specially selected as a good father for producing Guide Dog pups.

Derek Freeman was the person who, for 29 years, masterminded the association's entire breeding scheme. As well as choosing the stud

dogs and the brood bitches (the bitches kept specially for breeding Guide Dog pups) and deciding which dogs would mate with which bitches, Derek also organised the nation's puppy walkers — the people who volunteer to look after potential Guide Dog pups for the first year of their lives. We have been puppy walkers four times on Blue Peter.

If no suitable pups are bred, in the end there would be no Guide Dogs, so Derek is probably the man who has done more for Guide Dogs and their owners than any other single person in Britain.

Goldie's first litter, born in March 1981, had stud dog Danny as their father. There were five pups and we gave the only bitch, Lady, to Simon Groom's mum as a thank you for the help she had given to Blue Peter. Derek tested the others and said they could be puppy walked and you may remember Peter Duncan training Prince. Sadly, only two out of the four became Guide Dogs, the others just didn't

1. Douglas Field and Bruno.

2. Sheila Cramp and Fergie.

3. Pauline Allen and Amber.

4. Norah McGuire and Bonzo.

5. Lynda Drummond-Walker and Snowy.

6. Julia Simmons and Honey.

7. Derek Freeman and Halley.

Christmas cracker (bottom). Snowy stars on a Guide Dog card.

Newcomers (below) — Simon and Goldie.

have the right temperament, and one of them was too nervous of traffic. For Derek, this 50 per cent success rate just wasn't good enough. He decided Danny couldn't have been quite the right dog to mate with Goldie — although he had a fine record of producing excellent Guide Dog pups with other bitches. "I think I'll go for Zeke next time," he told us, after poring over loads of pedigree charts and family trees of dozens of dogs. "He's got a softer nature than Danny. He's a nice, kind dog and a solid, willing worker — maybe he'd be a better match with Goldie."

It was fascinating to know how important this matching of the two parents is. And not just how strong and well built they are, but their natures, too. If two highly strung dogs mate, the chances are their pups will be even more nervous. On the other hand, a Guide Dog must not be *too* placid. Derek was usually a wizard at matching — but would his plans for Goldie's second litter work out?

If you were watching Blue Peter last February you will know that they did. This time, Derek achieved 100 per cent success — with the help of Goldie and Zeke, of course!

Goldie had eight pups in her second litter — born on February 3rd, 1986. As everyone knows, we kept Bonnie to be our Blue Peter dog, because Goldie, her mum, retired from television when Simon Groom left the programme in 1987.

Derek tested the other seven and said that Bruno, Snowy, Fergie, Amber, Halley, Bonzo and Honey could all begin puppy walking.

Halley was such a magnificent looking dog Derek soon decided he should be earmarked as a stud — he had a perfect nature, too, and if all went well, would father hundreds of Guide Dogs, all with his fine body and gentle temperament. The rest continued to train and passed all their tests. And at a grand third birthday reunion in the Blue Peter studio, Bonnie was reunited with her seven clever brothers and sisters and the blind owners of the six that are Guide Dogs.

How did Derek feel about his seven out of seven score? "It's grand," he said. "They're a credit to their mum and dad." But he looked a little wistful all the same. "What's the matter Derek?" we asked. "Well," he replied, "I know you needed Bonnie for the programme, but I'm sure *she* would have been a great Guide Dog too!" No doubt Derek's right — and the score could well have been eight out of eight. But although she is not a pair of eyes for a blind person, Bonnie is giving great pleasure to millions of Blue Peter viewers all over Britain. That is very important too.

With seven pups working for the Guide Dogs for the Blind Association, and the eighth the most famous dog on TV, no wonder we call the litter Goldie's Wonders!

Now find a mirror!

Mystery Pix — Solutions

1 Yvette shakes hands with a life-size cardboard cut-out of a Hypsilophodon who roamed the earth 70 million years ago.

2 Mark with the King and Queen statue by Henry Moore. Valued at £2,000,000, the most precious object we have ever had in the Blue Peter studio.

3 Yvette climbing the Operation Innovator Bus mobile wall. The crane is holding our camera.

4 Table jugglers from the Peking Acrobats.

5 Five hundred Girl Guides from Hampshire West performing their song "Friends".

6 Mark tempting a baby Dama gazelle with a bottle of goat's milk.

7 Constructing the replica of the giant Woodchester Roman Pavement in the studio. At this point, three-quarters of the pavement is still missing.

8 That's Baldrick from Blackadder, alias Tony Robinson, underneath custard pies being thrown in aid of Comic Relief.

9 The enormous Spectrecolour electronic billboard celebrating Blue Peter's 30th birthday in Piccadilly Circus.

10 A giant Serpent brass instrument sold at Phillips for £5,000.

Useful information

Dogs for the Disabled
Brook House,
1 Lower Ladyes Hills,
Kenilworth,
Warwickshire CV8 2GN.
Telephone: 0926 59726.

Dan-Yr-Ogof Showcaves
Glyntawe,
Abercraf,
Near Swansea,
South Wales.
Telephone: 0639 730284

Royal Society for the Protection of Birds
The Lodge,
Sandy,
Bedfordshire SG19 2DL.
Telephone: 0767 80551.

Guide Dogs for the Blind Association
Alexandra House,
Park Street,
Windsor,
Berkshire SG4 1JR.
Telephone: 0753 855711.

Oxfam
274 Banbury Road,
Oxford OX2 7DZ.

The British Diabetic Association
10 Queen Anne Street,
London W1M 0BD.
Telephone: 01-323 1531.

If you want more recipes, you'll find them in these books:

The Diabetics Cookbook
Published by Dunitz
The Diabetic Kids' Cookbook
Published by Macdonald

Riding for the Disabled Association
Avenue 'R',
Agricultural Centre,
Kenilworth,
Warwickshire CV8 2LY.
Telephone: 0203 256107.

The Tales of Robin Hood
Maid Marian Way,
Nottingham NG11 6GF.
Telephone: 0602 414414.
Blue Peter Badge holders get in free!

Acknowledgements

Co-ordinator: *Anne Dixon*.
Designed by: *Judy Billson*.
Typeset by: *Area Graphics Ltd, Letchworth, Herts.*
Production: *Landmark Production Consultants Ltd, London.*
Colour separation by: *Fotographics Ltd, London & Hong Kong.*
Photographs were taken by:
Barry Boxall, John Ridley, John Green, Chris Capstick, John Jefford, Peter Lane, Dave Clarke, Phil Taylor, Robert Hill, Alex Leger, Nick Heathcote, Caroline Bacon, John Chapman, Vin Burnham, Des Stewart, M. Mackay — Frank Lane Picture Agency, Eckart Pott — Bruce Coleman Limited, Rex Features Limited, M.W. Richards — RSPB, You Magazine, Eric Hosking and Lewis Bronze.
Princess Beatrice photographs reproduced by gracious permission of Her Majesty The Queen.
The Baby Beas story was written by Dorothy Smith.
All Tied Up and Beastie Boxes by K.S. Video.

COMPETITION

Win a day out with Blue Peter!

THIS is your chance to win an all-expenses-paid V.I.P. visit to BBC Television Centre to meet us and see the Blue Peter programme being transmitted. It's a special prize because Blue Peter doesn't have a studio audience and only a select few get the chance to see us 'live'!

All you have to do is guess the answer to this question:

We started awarding Green Blue Peter badges on November 24th, 1988 — by July 1st, 1989, how many had been awarded?

Here's a clue — there are 5 digits in the answer.

The closing date is January 31st, 1990. Cut out your entry and send it to:

**Blue Peter Competition
BBC TV
London W12 7RJ.**

First prize winners and runners up will be notified by letter.

Age ....

Name ....
Address ....
The number of Green Blue Peter Badges is ....